MW00695277

HOW to Live your Life

India's most read writer on...

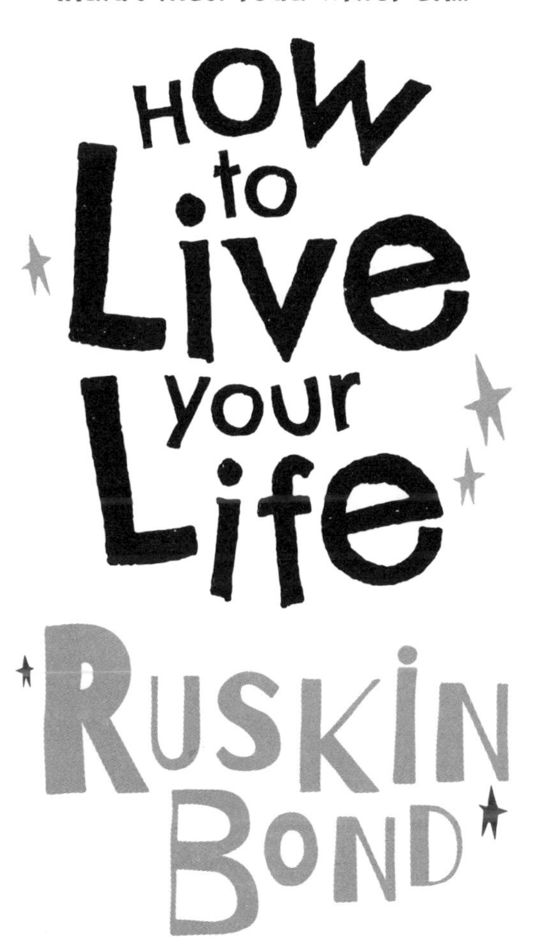

Illustrated & Designed by
Shamika Chaves

HarperCollins *Publishers* India

First published in India by HarperCollins Publishers 2022
Building No 10, Tower A, 4th Floor, DLF Cyber City, Phase II,
Gurugram – 122002

2 4 6 8 10 9 7 5 3 1

P-ISBN: 978-93-5629-226-0
E-ISBN: 978-93-5629-228-4

Cover design: **Shamika Chaves**
Author photo: **Siddharth Bond**

Typeset in **Merriweather, Regular, 9** by **Shamika Chaves**

Printed and bound at Lustra Print Process Pvt. Ltd.

HarperCollinsIn

CONTENTS

A letter from

Ruskin Bond

A Definition of Life

Dear Friends,

Yesterday was Basant.

Spring is here. That is, it has arrived in the plains, although up here in the hills it is still winter and I have just emerged from my razai and blanket in order to begin this letter.

The sun is up, its moving around on my bed and desk, and I must take advantage of its presence, because later my hands will be stiff with cold and holding a pen will be difficult.

Yes, I still write by hand. I've been doing it all my life and I don't see why I should stop now. I love the paper on which I write, I love the violet ink that flows from this gel pen, and I love the words that by some fusion of thought and action appear on this sunlit paper.

WORDS!

I HAVE LIVED FROM THEM FOR MOST OF MY LIFE AND I HOPE TO LIVE WITH THEM AND FROM THEM A LITTLE LONGER.
JUST A LITTLE LONGER.
I MUST NOT BE GREEDY.

I have, on the whole, had a wonderful life, and I will tell you more about it as we go along.

Starting the Day

First things first, and first of all I must thank all you, readers of all ages, for all the delightful letters you have written to me over the years – especially this past year, when we were all cooped up in our homes because of the coronavirus epidemic. And you wrote to me by hand, in your excellent handwriting, knowing that I did not use e-mail, message apps, and other technical aids.

No, I am not an enemy of progress. I am just a stubborn, old-fashioned Taurian, a bull who likes to graze in the meadows, who likes to be left alone and who might just charge at you if you disturb him while he's enjoying the sweet grass of summer.

And thank you for all your letters. If I was to reply to each one individually, I would be doing nothing else; and there's always a story to be finished and another to be started. Writers don't retire. Not this one, anyway. If I am to enjoy the sweet grass of summer, I must work for it.

I'm up with the lark, or rather, with the whistling thrush whose sweet notes ascend the mountain as I open my window to the sun's first morning rays. I let the sunshine run over my face, arms, chest. I close my eyes and allow the sun to dwell upon them for a minute or two.

Try it, my friend.
Don't open your eyes and
stare at the sun.
He'll stare back and you won't like it.
Just close your eyes and
take his blessings.
Then take a few deep breaths.
If you want to do a few exercises,
go ahead and do them,
they could loosen you up.

But don't force your
body into doing
something it doesn't
like.

Not everybody's body is the same. Some bodies like being stretched to the limit, and they will jog along the roads for miles. Some, like mine, are always looking for physical comfort and relaxation. I take my energy from the sun and the early morning air; I swing my arms around for a while, and kick an imaginary football. Then I sit down at my desk and write a few words.

I am doing it right now. The sun is on my writing hand, on the pad before me. On my left is a cheap desk clock, which tells me that there are still fifteen minutes to breakfast. When I was a nineteen-year old, living and working in London, I would often miss my breakfast (which I had to prepare myself) because I had to rush off to catch the train which would get me to my workplace in time. The result was malnutrition, poor vision and a month in the Hampstead General Hospital. Since then, I've never missed my breakfast.

Some of you like your parantha with a little pickle. So do I. Some of you like your idli and dosa. So do I. Some of you like a fried egg or an omelette. So do I. Some of you like porridge. I hate porridge! Enjoy your breakfast, my friend, and eat what you like most, because it's going to sustain you through the rest of the day. If you're a busy student or a working person, lunch will be a distraction, just some sabzi getting cold in a tiffin carrier. And if you go somewhere and indulge in a heavy lunch, you will have difficulty staying awake afterwards.

is important, my friend. Never miss your breakfast. Food is important but what has really sustained me all these years can be summed up in one word:

WORDS

If I did not have this half-hour to myself every morning – this half hour with my writing pad and the sun on my shoulder – I would be a grumpy and dissatisfied man for the rest of the day. An incomplete person. By putting down my early morning thoughts, feelings and observations, and in conveying them to you, invisible friend, I am, in some way, asserting my individuality and justifying my existence on this earth.

"Breakfast!" shouts Beena, my granddaughter, from the next room.

Further words of wisdom will have to wait till later in the day.

there's nothing worse than a fried egg gone cold

So here we are again.

I had mentioned the word talent.

Talent

If you have a talent, put it to some use.

It is something that some of us are born with; or even something that we might discover and acquire along the way.
I think most of you have it in some form or the other.

Occasionally, talent surfaces at an
early age.
You might discover that you can
draw
or
paint
rather well
or that you have a gift for
words
and putting them together;
or that when you
sing
people listen to you.
(I was always told to shut up.)
Or you might be good at figures,
or making things with your hands.

There's a
potential artist
or writer or singer
or musician in you.
or perhaps a
mathematician
or a toy-maker,
or a rocket maker.
or a juggler.

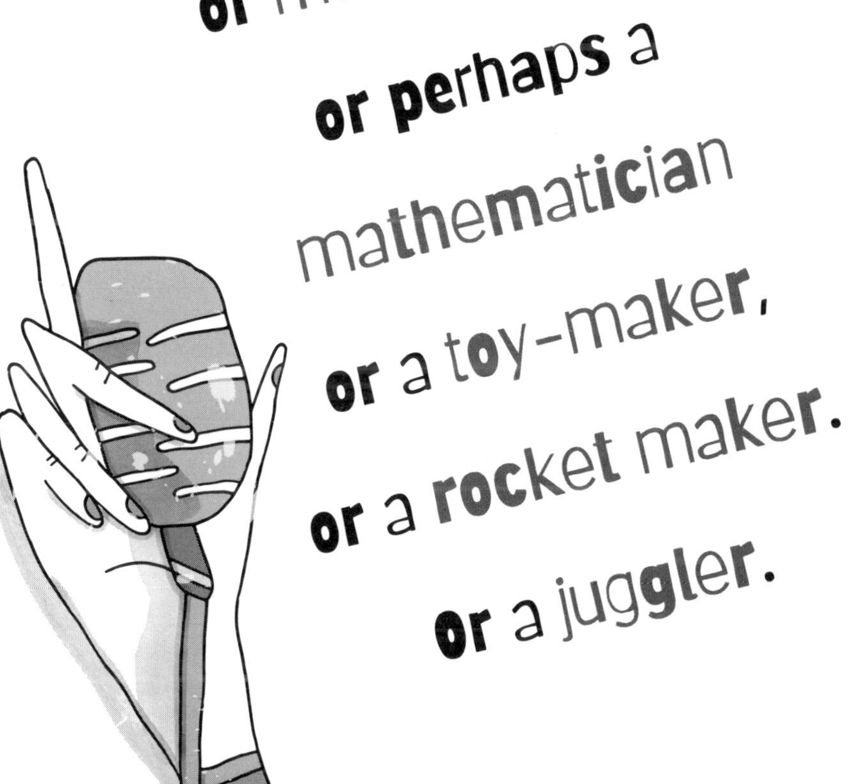

Shazam!

When I was a boy in prep school (circa 1943) we used that expression to describe something extraordinary that had just happened – like the school's main roof being blown away in a cyclonic storm (two days' holiday!), or an explosion in the science lab caused by a leaking gas tank, and the headmaster running out of his house in his underwear. Shazam!

Once you realize you have a talent, you must hang on to it, my friend. It has been given to you by God, or by Providence, or the DNA of your ancestors, and you must put it to good use in order to justify your presence on planet earth. It may take many years to become a successful artist or writer or singer or creative craftsman; it takes effort and commitment; but the goal is worth striving for. Move forward. Don't look back.

Sometimes our parents or guardians saddle us with their ambitions - what they would like us to be, rather than what we'd like to be.

When I came home after completing my school education, my mother asked me what I was thinking of in terms of a profession or career.

"I think I'm going to be a writer," I said. "Don't be silly," was her response, "you should join the Army!"

Now, the Army is a great service and a career too if you want to become a General with (or without) a fierce moustache, and in 1950 it was almost every schoolboy's first choice. But it was not for a dreamy fellow like me, who spent most of his free time with his head buried in a book of verse or a novel or an encyclopedia of natural history.

Parade and early morning P.T. were not for me. I could not even load my stepfather's guns let alone fire them. I shuddered at the touch of one of these weapons. And yet I was quite happy reading John Buchan's *The Thirty-Nine Steps*, or Graham Greene's *This Gun for Hire*, or any thriller packed with murder and mayhem. **I lived vicariously through the characters in books and stories.** So why not write a few?

Do what you are good at, that has always been my advice. If you can sing, sing your heart out; sing to the world, and the world will reward your singing. If you can dance, dance your way to the stars, and become a star. If you can play the tabla, then tabla your way to glory! If you can paint, become another Gauguin, another Jamini Roy. If you can visualize a story, a screenplay, aim to be another Satyajit Ray, a Renoir, a Benegal. If you can act, be an actor. If you are better behind the camera, be a great cameraman. Be a camera!

be whatever you want to be

Give it your heart and soul,

and you will have made something

of your life, my friend.

You are all my sons and

daughters when it comes

to telling you

HOW TO LIVE YOUR LIFE.

Not all of us have artistic natures. My best friend at school, a German Boy called Kaspa Kirschner, became a famous scientist in his native land. A Parsi friend became a successful hotelier. A Sikh friend went to England and at present owns the largest wine shop in the country; another became the Samosa King of South London.

Up here, on Mussoorie's Mall Road, there is nearly always a line of people waiting their turn outside a small shop where the owner makes nothing but omelettes. But his omelettes are the best between the Mall and New Delhi, and he is justly famous for them.

Even making the perfect omelette takes skill, commitment, even love. Giving satisfaction, giving pleasure, that is often a reward in itself. I can boil an egg. But I can't make a decent omelette.

I can add and subtract but that doesn't make me a magician or a mathematician.

I can sing (preferably when no one is listening) but that doesn't make me a Tansen or a Caruso or a Mohit Chauhan.

I can draw an apple, but that doesn't make me a Van Gogh.

But I can write! I can put words together. I can make a story, a poem, a word picture. And I've done it all my life, and made it my justification for being here.

And there's something special you can do, even if you are not as yet quite sure what it could be. It's lurking there somewhere in the back of your mind. It will come to the fore one of these days. And then you can forge ahead. And don't look back.

Don't Look Back

Don't look back at failure.

Our past is full of regrets, of things that bother us from time to time. As you get older, you will look back at your boyhood, girlhood, teens, and wish that you had done things differently at certain times. Don't let these memories stand in your way.

Face them, and put them aside.

I regret quarrelling with my mother.

I regret neglecting my sister.

I regret failing an exam. I regret being rude to one of my teachers. I regret letting down a friend. I regret breaking the classroom windows. In other words, I was a horrible boy. But I admit to all these failures, and I carry on trying to be a better person.

It rained last night. After a dry spell lasting a couple of months, there has finally been a shower, and there is a freshness in the air that has been missing for some time.

I open my window, take a deep breath. Take several deep breaths. I'm told deep breathing is good for the heart and lungs. I'm not a great one for early morning exercise, but I'll go along with deep breathing and the extra oxygen that comes with it.

If you can start the day well, the rest of the day will usually follow in a calm and resolute fashion.

Don't Sleep Late If You Can Help It.

I'm up at six, not to go jogging, but simply to see that pink and orange glow as first light begins to spread over the mountains. When it has gone, I get back into bed (it's still cold late February) and wait for the dawn light to spread, and then, at six, for the sun to come leaping over the mountains and charging into my room. Shazam!

Then I crawl into a sitting position, reach for this little pad and my gel-pen with it's jamun-coloured ink, and start writing. Maybe it's a story, maybe a poem, maybe this letter to you.

Something, anything, but I must write.

My vision isn't as good as it used to be, but this early morning light is helpful, and the sun on my writing hand, helps to loosen up my fingers. Sunshine always helps. That's why we are here, alive and still singing.

I write for half an hour, and then I am ready to face the day.

Sometimes we have to
face the day. Face problems,
obstacles, shortages (money
shortages, usually), enmity,
quarrelsome people, leaking roofs,
the milkman missing, a mad
monkey terrorizing school children,
a loudspeaker too loud, rats making a
nest in the television set
(it's of some use after all),
and running out of pyjamas.
We must face all these
calamities and difficulties
with equanimity.

Finding Nature

And then I sit down and write an ode to my geraniums ...

Geraniums! What a difference they have made to my life. Whenever I have felt depressed, or a little down in the dumps, I have gone to my little sun-room where I have been growing geraniums for several years. They are a riot of colour for most of the year – deep pink, pillar-box red, snow white, cerise – and when I gaze upon them, I feel better, more capable of dealing with the stresses of the day.

GROW SOMETHING, MY FRIEND.

Even if it's only a succulent
or a feathery fern.
Find some corner of your room or
balcony or window ledge where
there's a little sun, good light and
warmth; plant a seed or cutting;
watch it grow; watch it flower.
You will *have* taken a small part in
God's creation, and the rewards
will be greater than the effort you
have made.

If you have space around your dwelling, make a garden. If you are a landowner, plant trees, grow a forest! Become one of Nature's allies, not one of her enemies. There are enough people around who are only too willing to do away with forests, meadows, lakes, wild creatures, the green of this unique planet. Join those who wish to preserve it.

So I repeat. Grow something; give something back to Mother Earth. She gives us everything we need in order to survive – food, pure water, clean air... let's give something back, even if it's only a climbing bean on the window ledge.

"A beanfield full in blossom smells as sweet," wrote the poet John Clare, and I'm sure there would be more love on this earth if we grew flowers, instead of guns.

In Bhutan, they grow sunflowers. I saw them all the way from the airport to the capital Thimphu. These open-faced flowers are aptly named. They turn their heads to face the sun because, like us, they are the children of the sun. They resemble their parent. Each flower produces hundreds of seeds, each one life-giving. Given space, they will multiply. Each seed gives us edible oil, nutrition.

Give them space.

Give
Nature
A Little Love,
And It Will Be
Returned A
Hundred-Fold.
Give It Concrete,
These Structures Must
Sooner Or Later
Turn To Rubble.
The Ruins Of
Earlier Civilizations
Are There For
All To See.

Love

Love.

Now that's a word to conjure with. It has so many aspects: love for one's offspring, a very natural mother's love, and quite often a father's! Love for one's parents – this can vary according to family circumstances. Then there's love for one's friends – a very noble love, for it is not based on a blood relationship. There is also passionate love – based on a fine chemistry, in which two individuals are drawn to each other physically and mentally, and often for no logical reason!

Two people, whose natures and backgrounds are totally different, are attracted to each other, feel a need for each other, and want to walk hand in hand through the rest of their lives, come what may.

Of course, it doesn't always work so perfectly. Sometimes that tremendous surge of love for another isn't mutual. Doesn't it happen to most of us, at some time in our youth or growing or adult years.
We love someone tenderly, deeply, selflessly, but our feelings are not reciprocated. The loved one does not feel the same way about us! We are cast aside, left heart-broken.

What are we to do about it? Go on living in anguish? Become a stalker? Contemplate suicide?

Do nothing, my friend.

is the greatest *healer*.

And the *human* mind is adaptable.

The horrible days pass.

The lonely *weeks* pass.

The angry, self-pitying months pass by, suddenly it's a new year, and a lot is happening around you, and you are winning prizes and displaying your talents, and perhaps you are at a party in a crowded room, and there, across this crowded room, you see a face, someone you have never seen before, and her eyes, or his meet yours, and there is the recognition of a kindred soul.

Behold, a stranger! But someone you have been searching for all your life.

Some enchanted evening, across a crowded room... you will see a stranger and your life will be changed in seconds!

Nothing
is predictable
in this journey
through a life where
everyone makes
Predictions.
What the stars foretell
is strictly for astrologers.

Chance gives,
and takes away,
and gives again.

And then there is self-love.

Beware of self-love.

It's fine to take pride in your appearance and achievements, but once you start feeling that you are superior to others, smarter than them, better than them in every way, you are in danger of becoming a very unpleasant person, a potential dictator, a little Hitler in fact.

Look into the mirror when you have to, but don't spend hours in front of it, preening yourself, and falling in love with your own image. Your image will change with time, and then you will fall out of love with yourself and become a bitter person.

"Nobody loves me."

And that's the other extreme, a feeling that you're not wanted, of no importance and of no use to anyone. We wallow in self-pity. We give way to depression.

Depression. It can lead to extremes – to drugs and suicidal moods and actions. Depression can be the result of repeated failures. But it can also be the result of too much success and an inability to handle it. We cannot be at the top all the time. The graph of success reaches a peak, and then it drops – slowly in most cases, but rapidly in others. It's the rapid decline that is hard to take.

Of course, many of us go through life without the stimulus of fame and fortune. We adapt, we shift our targets, we change course. Small achievements usually last longer than spectacular accomplishments.

A healthy body and an enquiring mind are all that most of us need.

Shake off that fit of depression. Go for a walk. Look at the busy people on the street, in the shops, in the fields. Are they depressed? They don't have time for it.

Time and Life

TIME PASSES VERY SWIFTLY. DON'T ALLOW IT TO LEAVE YOU TOO FAR BEHIND.

Make a friend.

Find friends.

Join a group of people

who are doing interesting things.

Some of the most balanced

people I know are

Bird

Watchers.

Yes, bird-watchers. They get together at the crack of dawn, go tramping along into the fields and forests and surrounding countryside looking for rare birds, colourful birds, beautiful birds, and they make notes and take pictures, and they are full of excitement when they see something special, some great work of nature.

Sometimes these enthusiasts will even disguise themselves as bushes so that they can get closer to their avian friends.

Be a bush! I tried it myself once, when I was younger, and everyone agreed that I looked better as a bush than as a tubby writer.

Other well-balanced people include gardeners, collectors (of books, stamps, colourful pebbles, anything!), sketch-pad artists, zoo-keepers, archaeologists... they are all doing something which combines work and pleasure.

Cooks are usually well-balanced too. Often having to cook for large numbers of people (in hotels, in army camps, on ships), they get used to witnessing the foibles of the human race while helping to sustain it.

and the more you look outwards,

the better you will feel inwardly.

In the old days, when a mutiny broke out on a ship, it was usually the cook who survived. Captains were dispensable, cooks are always required. Shipwrecked sailors sometimes became cannibals, but even then, a little flavouring and garnishing is necessary, so the cook will be the last to be cooked – if there's anyone left to cook him!

Enough of cannibals and curried captains.

There is a noticeable absence of humour in today's world. Humourous writers stay away from politics. Cartoonists get into trouble if they make fun of men in power. I miss the cartoons of R.K Laxman, the iconic humour of his brother, R.K Narayan's stories of Malgudi. I miss the humour of James Thurber in *The New Yorker*. I miss the satire of Evelyn Waugh in novels such as *Scoop* and *Decline and Fall*. We have a very funny writer in Jug Suraiya, who has a column in *The Times of India*, but he is funny at his own expense.

Life is too serious
to be taken
seriously. We need
a little humour.
Sometimes we must
see the funny side
of things if we are
not to lose our
sanity. Well, it's
good to laugh at
oneself – and safer
than laughing at
others!

Gautam, my grandson, who is always interested in new inventions, tells me that a machine has just been invented in the USA which is guaranteed to make you feel "calm and happy". It's a helmet of sorts, he tells me, and when you wear it, a current of pure happiness will pass through your brain. An end to all stress and worry!

I find it rather depressing.

If we are all going to go about our lives in a state of "calm and complete happiness", we will become a bunch of lotus-eaters, happy to do nothing, gazing benignly upon the suffering and starving millions, and ignoring our own friends and family.

It's worry that makes the world go round, and when we stop worrying about ourselves and about others, it means we have given up on the struggle to survive.

•

Put on your "happy helmet", forget your problems, and let the world collapse around you.

•

No, it's the worriers who achieve something in this life.

•

They worry and they do something about it.

•

And they celebrate.

Celebrations

SHAZAM!

Celebrations!

There is much to celebrate –

just being alive, to begin with.

Being aware of being alive. Most of the time we take our little lives for granted, almost as though we are doing this planet a favour by raising our dwellings, our towering apartments, upon it. But this planet was alive and brimming with all kinds of plant and animal life long before our ancestors came into existence. We have inherited this green place and done our best to disfigure it.

There is much to be saved –
rivers and streams,
mountains and forests,
birds and butterflies,
big whales and small fish,
plants of all kinds,
tribal folk, nomads, camels,
crocodiles, cockatoos!
Come my friends, there's all this natural wealth still with us. Let's celebrate it, let's preserve it. It's your inheritance, why throw it away?

Once a year we celebrate our individual birthdays.

On that one day in the year we do sometimes realize how lucky we are to be alive.

And yet, surely, every day is a birthday – a birthday for you and me and the night watchman even if he has just fallen asleep with the rising of the sun. Some of us must work by night, and some, like the wise owl and the crafty jackal, do most of their living by night.

But when the night has passed, the sun comes shouting over the mountains, and it's saying...

"It's another day, another Birthday, for you and me and the rest of the world." And the birds burst into song, and the grass bathes in the morning dew, and the peepal leaves dance in the morning breeze, and you open your eyes and yawn and get ready for school or college or place of work, and the world is out there waiting for you to say something.

Say it, my friend.

Happy Birthday, World!

That place of work.

Anti-climax.

Get on with it, Bond. Finish that story.

Sneha, have you done your homework?

Kirinsmith, have you finished your project?

Mr. Mistry, you have a speech to prepare.

Pradeep, don't forget your car keys and wallet.

You have a train to catch, a bus to board, a plane about to take off, a car with an empty petrol tank, a scooter in need of repair. Hurry, hurry! Everyone's on the move – some to study or prepare ourselves for the years ahead; most of us to earn a few rupees, or possibly even pounds or dollars or whatever it is the Arabs use. And although you and I would love to join that parrot in the mango tree, feasting on that luscious golden fruit, we must put it off till the weekend or a holiday, or — memory, hold the door — that wonderful day when I played truant from school and spent all day in a litchi tree.

That was a long time ago. I did it just once. And I was fined a week's pocket money. I remember that time with some affection. We have to get up to mischief occasionally. But not too often, my friend.

There's work to be done. And a little hard work does nobody any harm. It has kept me going all these years — from my teens into my old age. I haven't overdone it, I take a nap whenever I feel like it, but I'm no tortoise either. There's a time to run,

and there's a time to lie on
the grass and munch lettuce
leaves. Sometimes the hare,
sometimes the tortoise. The
tortoise may have won that
race, but if the house was
burning down, who would you
send for the fire-engine – the
tortoise or the hare?

When you know what to do with yourself, when you know what you want to do with your life, take a deep breath – take several deep breaths – and get down to hard work that will lay the foundation for your success, for the flowering of your talents. You will enjoy your work if you are good at it. You may feel discouraged by a few failures, but if you are good you won't be distracted by them, you will simply try out your ideas in a different way.

Ideas

Ideas!
Combine ideas
with talent and
hard work, and you have genius.
You have Madame Curie
discovering radium and putting it to use.
You have Louis Pasteur and his anti-rabies vaccine;
you have Alexander Fleming discovering penicillin;
Einstein splitting the atom, and an unknown genius
inventing the samosa.
The application of ideas to the
requirements of mankind;
I suppose that's the
right definition.

Unfortunately, some men of science become slaves to their political leaders, and use their talents to create weapons of mass destruction. There is always the danger that science will be wrongly applied; that one will be enslaved by technology or by the misuse of drugs that were meant to save lives.

But I have no wish to lecture you. If you have ideas, you are on your way to achieving great things. There is no limit to new discoveries, new fashions, new ways to serve old dishes.

Let us for a spell, get away from the serious business of making a living or making a mark in life. If I were to go on about it, you wouldn't finish reading this letter, you would consign it to the wastepaper basket or the litter bin. And rightly so. Because if we are to spend all our lives burning the midnight oil and striving to be one step ahead of all our friends and families, we might as well shoot ourselves in the head. As some have done, out of an excess of ambition and a failure to reach the standards we have imposed on ourselves.

If we can't be happy on this amazing planet, there's no point in hanging around, is there?
Heaven, if not mars, beckons.

We need to be happy at least some of the time, and while some simple souls have learnt the trick of being happy, more complicated minds have failed to do so. Hamlet, who thought too much, was miserable, and made everyone else miserable. Quixote, who put aside thought, was happiest when tilting at windmills. Thoreau, who thought a good deal, found happiness in keeping human company to a minimum. Dickens, equally thoughtful, revelled in human company.

To each his own...

No two minds are alike. No two roses are alike. No two kisses are the same.

EACH OF US
SEEKS HAPPINESS
IN HIS OR HER
OWN WAY,
AND THE EASIEST
WAY OF FINDING
IT IS NOT TO
SEARCH FOR IT
AT ALL.
LET IT COME TO YOU.

Pursue the butterfly and it will fly away. Stay still for a few moments and it might just settle on your hand. Stillness is everything. The Buddha taught us the value of stillness. So did the great saints and recluses in their mountain abodes. Alone, but never lonely. For when you merge with the forces of nature, you become one with nature, and you are as much a rock or tree as the ones that surround you.

Relax, my friend. I am not urging you to leave your home and become a recluse on a lonely mountain-top. Only a few great souls can achieve that elevation of the spirit.

Does that sound complicated? It does a little, I think, and I don't want to confuse you.

'Simplify, simplify!' as Thoreau would say, living in a hut near a desolate pond in the wilderness. No electricity, no smart phone. I wouldn't miss the phone (I am still without one), but I'd miss the things I'm used to having: the morning newspaper, the call of the postman (as opposed to the call of the bulbul), a constant supply of books, the occasional walk to the coffee house (as opposed to the walk to the pond for a bucket of water), and a ceiling fan to keep away the mosquitoes. It's hard to get a good night's sleep when bats, rats, and wild cats are all trying to share your cabin with you.

Your list of necessities would be longer than mine, I'm sure, since you're a twenty-first century person, and you'll miss your motorcycle – or your make-up box.

The more intimate
you are with the
natural world –
the world that
exists without
actually having
to worry about
how to exist –
the more we will
be able to come
to terms with
our own natures.

I would recommend a week in the wilderness and then back to the comforts of your 17th floor apartment in Noida. After all, nature isn't going anywhere. It's still out there, beyond the marketplace, the national highway, the river of cars and trucks, the industrial areas, the wayside eateries, the villages now towns, the towns now cities, it's out there somewhere and you can find it if you make the effort. And when the cities grow old and the mountains crumble, nature returns – slowly, but surely – and you will find dandelions growing in the walls, daisies in the doorsteps, and peepal trees where there were rooftops.

To be honest, we need a little of both worlds.

Wild Sorrel.

Driving down to Dehra (or rather, being driven down), even at some speed, I couldn't help noticing the bunches of pink sorrel, thriving on the otherwise bare hillsides and even growing on the road's retaining walls. At this time of the year it's in flower – pink confetti – but it survives all the year round, in the most inhospitable places. The hill folk call it 'Almora grass' probably because of its presence there, but it's common all over the Western Himalayas, and as schoolboys, both in Shimla and Mussoorie, we would eat the sweet and sour flowers; but not too many, or we would be rushing off to the loo. Granny would sometimes add a little sorrel to her soups, for flavouring, so it had its uses. And, like most wild plants, it binds the soil together and prevents it from being washed away during the heavy monsoon rains.

Tenacity is a quality that we could all do with; that is, the ability to continue to do something for longer than might be expected. In other words, don't give up easily. Finish that project. Complete that task. Finish that race even if you are coming in last. Stick with your ambitions; work towards them. Hold on to life, to that steep mountain slope. There's always something you can do.

We have to zig-zag a little.

We see more of the world that way, and the world sees more of us. If one approach doesn't work, try another. If you can't sing well, learn to speak well. If you can't speak well, learn to write well, or maybe you can paint or dance, or make a rocket, or sail a boat, or fly an aeroplane, or drive a steam-roller, or grow french beans, or make an omelette.

There's a man in this town who's become quite famous because of his omelettes. He has a little shop on the Mall. When I write a story, I think of it as an omelette. The right ingredients, just the right amount of cooking, and the right amount of love.

A little love makes
for a great omelette,
a great pudding, a
great story, a great
film, a great musical,
a great invention, a
great human-being.
Just a little love, my
friend, makes all the
difference in the end.

There's a West Indian proverb which goes, 'Every day no Christmas, an' every day no rainy day'.

A philosophical attitude, implying that we must take each day as it comes, and wait for the weather to clear up, before bringing out the cricket gear.

The weather won't stop you from doing the calypso, and I remember a Christmas in London, long ago, when I joined some Jamaican friends for a Christmas party, and the dancing went on all night even though it was snowing outside.

Dance on an island in the sun, when the sun is out. But you can sing in the rain too, and one very hot summer in the plains, when the first rains came, we ran out on the flat roof and sang and danced with gay abandon.

'Just singin' in the rain ...
I'm happy again!'

I'm the world's most tuneless singer, but try stopping me when I feel like singing!

We burst into song when we are brimful of happiness. Can't help it actually. And sometimes, when we are feeling low or a little depressed, a good remedy is to start singing. "When you are down and out, stand up and shout – it's going to be a great day!" The human voice is unique in that it can convey a variety of emotions and communicate in hundreds of languages. Dogs can bark and birds can sing, but we can say most anything!

Life and Luck

TREAT EVERY DAY AS THOUGH IT'S THE MOST IMPORTANT DAY OF YOUR LIFE. THAT SOUNDS SIMPLE ENOUGH, BUT ACTUALLY IT ISN'T. THIS DAY, TODAY, BRINGS WITH IT THE BURDEN OF ALL THE DAYS, ALL THE MONTHS, ALL THE YEARS THAT HAVE GONE BEFORE, AND YOU HAVE TO CARRY THAT BURDEN INTO THE NEXT DAY AND THE YEARS TO COME.

It's easier to handle if you are in your teens or twenties, because at that age you can recover quickly from setbacks and failures. And I know you will, my friend.

When I was fifty, I decided I was a failure. I had made a living, my writings had been published, I was in reasonably good health; but somehow as an author, my career hadn't really taken off. I was just an "also ran", and I felt it was better not to run at all than to be an "also ran".

And then a publisher disinterred an early work of mine, my first novel, and presented it to a new and younger generation, and to my surprise it took off and was the precursor to many more literary successes.

Pure luck, you could say.

We All Need A Little **Luck.**
And It Will Come If We Give
It A **Chance.** If We Have
Something To Show For All
The Years Of **Hard Work**
And **Commitment.** So It's
Important To **Run,** To Be An
"Also Ran" For As Long As
We Have To, And Then To
Sprint Ahead When We Get
Our **Second** Or **Third Wind.**

But life is not a race.

How can it be? Are we in a race against time, against the coming of old age? We are given a certain number of years on this revolving sphere, and we must revolve with it or perish. If you're in too much of a hurry, like Napolean, you'll end up on St. Helena, conversing with his ghost. Better to be a bull in a field of buttercups, searching for the grass that's sweetest.

We must look for our own meadow, that little place where happiness lurks, and if we don't ask for too much we might indeed find it – the hill of our dreams. Don't ask for the mountain, you won't be able to hold it up. Don't ask for the ocean, you will be lost in its depths. Take the mountain stream, the gently sloping hill, the sheltered bay, the singing sands.

The Race Is Not To Be WON, It's To Be RUN.

SHAZAM!

You asked me for a letter and I've given you an epistle.

You asked me for a definition of life, and instead of a simple soft-boiled egg, I've given you a scrambled egg. Or what, as a boy, I called a "rumble-tumble".

"Dad, make me a rumble-tumble," I would call out, and he would dutifully break a couple of eggs, stir them up with "sugar and spice and everything nice", and present me with the glorious result, what we now call an egg-bhurji.

These little childhood memories, especially the innocent ones, stay with us into our twilight years. A remembrance of the good times, the better things in life, help to make the journey worth the effort.

I have gone on quite a bit about the joys of daybreak, bird song, the sun coming up, a new beginning, a good breakfast, and a good day's work; but I haven't said much about the close of the day, a time of rest and recollection, the coming of evening, the world's brief twilight, and the moon coming up over the mountains.

Where have all the birds gone? Suddenly they are silent. A multitude of mynas, gossiping in the mango grove, have gone to sleep all at once. It's bedtime for the birds, parents and children alike. There's no TV to keep them up late.

Only the wise owl, like a chowkidar, will stay up most of the night, on the lookout for an unwary mouse. He'll sleep by day, like some of us.

The night is my friend, it always has been. It brings a little magic into our lives.

A firefly floats in from the open window. A small moth is drawn towards the bed lamp, flutters around it. The neighbourhood cat slips into my room, curls up at the foot of my bed. Outside a nightjar calls.

Don't be afraid of
the dark, my friend.
We are not alone.
Those who have
gone are still with
us, enshrined in our
memories.
We feel their
presence, even as
the night wind
rustles the curtains.

I go to the window. Now the stars are out, millions of them strung across the Milky Way. How can we be lonely? So many stars out there! The cat looks up at them, starlight in her golden eyes. Perhaps she knows something about them that we don't. Wisdom is not the prerogative of human beings. It's out there, in the creative force that made this world.

DON'T BE AFRAID
OF LIFE.
IT'S OUT THERE,
YOURS TO DO WITH
AS YOU WISH.
TAKE IT.
CHERISH IT.

And with that,

I'll end this letter.

With bonds of love,

I remain,

Yours truly,

P. S. : Shazam!

Photos: **Siddharth Bond**

About the Author

RUSKIN BOND

is one of India's most well-known writers. He was awarded the **Padma Shri** in **1999** and the **Padma Bhushan** in **2014**.
He lives in Landour, Mussoorie.
Ruskin Bond's other books with **HarperCollins** include, **'These Are A Few Of My Favourite Things'**, **'Koki's Song'** and **'How To Be A Writer'**.

About the Illustrator

SHAMIKA CHAVES

is a children's book illustrator, author and graphic designer who's based in Mumbai. She successfully pursued a degree in applied art and has worked on several children's books. She has also worked as a comic artist and enjoys character design and hand type. Most recently she was shortlisted for **Publishing Next's** coveted **'Illustrator Of The Year 2021'** award. Shamika lives and works in a cosy little home with her husband, Christopher and their eight-year-old tortoise, Sebastian. Visit **@shamikasdoodles** on Instagram to learn more about her work.

HOW TO BE A WRITER

"Wherever I go, I meet young writers, or young people who want to write, and they are always asking questions. Someone who has survived as a writer for seventy years must have something to offer by way of "tips" (as one young friend put it) or the lessons learnt from all the ups and downs of a literary journey."

How To Be A Writer is peppered with nuggets of practical advice for every person who is aspiring to write and be published – all told in Ruskin Bond's characteristic understated, tongue-in-cheek, humorous style.

So, what is it that a person requires the most to become a writer? A love of books, of language, of life, an observant eye and a good memory along with enthusiasm, optimism and persistence.

How To Be A Writer is an exclusive glimpse into the writing credo of Ruskin Bond, an author who has had an incredibly successful writing career spanning over 70 years.